The New Mushroom Cookbook

Delicious Mushroom Recipes for Every Meal

By
BookSumo Press

D1396661

Published by
BookSumo Press,
http://www.booksumo.com/

About the Author.

BookSumo Press is a publisher of unique, easy, and healthy cookbooks.

Our cookbooks span all topics and all subjects. If you want a deep dive into the possibilities of cooking with any type of ingredient. Then BookSumo Press is your go to place for robust yet simple and delicious cookbooks and recipes. Whether you are looking for great tasting pressure cooker recipes or authentic ethic and cultural food. BookSumo Press has a delicious and easy cookbook for you.

With simple ingredients, and even simpler step-by-step instructions BookSumo cookbooks get everyone in the kitchen chefing delicious meals.

BookSumo is an independent publisher of books operating in the beautiful Garden State (NJ) and our team of chefs and kitchen experts are here to teach, eat, and be merry!

INTRODUCTION

Welcome to *The Effortless Chef Series*! Thank you for taking the time to purchase this cookbook.

Come take a journey into the delights of easy cooking. The point of this cookbook and all BookSumo Press cookbooks is to exemplify the effortless nature of cooking simply.

In this book we focus on Mushrooms. You will find that even though the recipes are simple, the taste of the dishes are quite amazing.

So will you take an adventure in simple cooking? If the answer is yes please consult the table of contents to find the dishes you are most interested in.

Once you are ready, jump right in and start cooking.

— BookSumo Press

TABLE OF CONTENTS

Any Issues? Contact Us

If you find that something important to you is missing from this book please contact us at info@booksumo.com.

We will take your concerns into consideration when the 2nd edition of this book is published. And we will keep you updated!

— BookSumo Press

Legal Notes

COMMON ABBREVIATIONS

cup(s)	C.
tablespoon	tbsp
teaspoon	tsp
ounce	oz.
pound	lb.

*All units used are standard American measurements

CHAPTER 1: EASY MUSHROOM RECIPES

VITO'S AWARD WINNING LINGUINE

Ingredients

- 1 lb. linguine, cooked al dente, drain
- 6 tbsp butter
- 10 cloves garlic, minced
- 6 C. mushrooms, sliced
- 1 tsp dried basil
- 1/4 tsp salt
- pepper
- 2 tbsp olive oil
- 2 tbsp parsley, chopped
- parmesan cheese, grated

Directions

- Prepare the pasta by following the instructions on the package.
- Place a pan over medium heat. Heat in it 2 tbsp of butter. Cook in them the garlic with mushroom, basil, a pinch of salt and pepper.
- Let them cook for 6 to 8 min until they become soft. Stir in the olive oil with the rest of the butter.
- Turn off the heat. Stir in the linguine. Serve it warm.
- Enjoy.

Servings per Recipe: 4

Timing Information:

Preparation	10 mins
Total Time	25 min

Nutritional Information:

Calories	670.7
Fat	26.1g
Cholesterol	45.8mg
Sodium	312.1mg
Carbohydrates	91.2g
Protein	18.8g

* Percent Daily Values are based on a 2,000 calorie diet.

Italian Mozzarella and Bacon Stuffed Mushrooms

Ingredients

- 1 lb. mushroom
- 3 slices turkey bacon, chopped
- 1/2 C. chopped onion
- 1 clove garlic, chopped
- 1 C. shredded mozzarella cheese
- 1/2 C. soft breadcrumbs
- 1/4 tsp oregano
- 1/4 tsp salt

Directions

- Before you do anything, preheat the oven to 375 F.
- Cut off the mushroom stems and chop them. Place the mushroom caps aside.
- Place a pan over medium heat. Heat in it a splash of oil.
- Cook in it the garlic with onion, mushroom stems, bacon, a pinch of salt and pepper.
- Let them cook for 6 min. Add the rest of the ingredients. Let them cook to make the filling.
- Spoon the filling into the mushroom caps. Place them on a baking sheet.
- Place the pan in the oven and let them cook for 11 min.
- Sprinkle some cheese on top then cook them for an extra 2 min.
- Serve your cheesy mushroom caps warm.
- Enjoy.

Servings per Recipe: 1

Timing Information:

Preparation	20 mins
Total Time	30 mins

Nutritional Information:

Calories	18.3
Fat	1.0g
Cholesterol	2.9mg
Sodium	46.4mg
Carbohydrates	1.0g
Protein	1.2g

* Percent Daily Values are based on a 2,000 calorie diet.

SIMPLE JAPANESE STIR-FRIED MUSHROOMS

Ingredients

- 1 tbsp butter
- 2 cloves garlic, minced
- 1 1/2 lbs. mushrooms, sliced
- 1/4 C. soy sauce
- garlic powder
- black pepper

Directions

- Get a mixing bowl: Heat in it the butter until it melts.
- Sauté in it the garlic for 2 to 3 min. Stir in the mushroom and cook them for 5 min.
- Add the soy sauce with garlic powder, a pinch of salt and pepper. Let them cook for 11 min.
- Serve your mushroom stir fry warm with some rice.
- Enjoy.

Servings per Recipe: 4

Timing Information:

Preparation	10 mins
Total Time	30 mins

Nutritional Information:

Calories	76.0
Fat	3.4g
Cholesterol	7.6mg
Sodium	1039.6mg
Carbohydrates	7.0g
Protein	7.2g

* Percent Daily Values are based on a 2,000 calorie diet.

4-INGREDIENT STUFFED WHITE BUTTONS

Ingredients

- 2 (12 oz.) packages white button mushrooms
- 1 (8 oz.) packages cream cheese
- 1 (8 oz.) packages sausage
- 1/4 C. butter

Directions

- Before you do anything, preheat the oven to 350 F.
- Clean the mushroom and rinse them. Drain them and cut of the stems. Chop the mushroom caps and place them aside.
- Place a pan over medium heat. Cook in it the sausage for 5 min. Stir in the chopped stems with garlic.
- Let them cook for 3 min. discard the excess fat.
- Get a mixing bowl: Stir in it the cream cheese with the sausage mixture to make the filling.
- Grease a baking dish with some batter. Place in it the mushroom caps with the hollow side facing up.
- Spoon the spoon the filling into the caps. Pour some water on the side enough to cover the base of the pan.
- Place it in the oven and let it cook for 32 to 46 min. Serve you mushroom casserole warm.
- Enjoy.

Servings per Recipe: 6

Timing Information:

Preparation	30 mins
Total Time	1 hr 10 mins

Nutritional Information:

Calories	343.2
Fat	31.8g
Cholesterol	83.9mg
Sodium	539.1mg
Carbohydrates	6.1g
Protein	10.3g

* Percent Daily Values are based on a 2,000 calorie diet.

How to Fry Mushrooms

Ingredients

- 10 oz. white mushrooms, wiped clean
- 1 C. flour
- 1/2 C. cornstarch
- 3/4 tsp baking powder
- 1/4 tsp salt
- 1 C. water
- 2 C. breadcrumbs

Directions

- Get a mixing bowl: Stir in it the flour, cornstarch, baking powder and salt.
- Pour in the water and whisk them until no lumps are found.
- Place a deep pan over medium heat. Heat in it about 1/2 inch of oil.
- Stick a toothpick into a mushroom. Dip it in the flour batter then roll it in the breadcrumbs.
- Repeat the process with several other mushrooms then cook them in the hot oil until they become golden brown.
- Drain the fried mushrooms and place them aside. Repeat the process with the remaining mushrooms.
- Serve them with your favorite dip.
- Enjoy.

Servings per Recipe: 3

Timing Information:

Preparation	15 mins
Total Time	25 mins

Nutritional Information:

Calories	538.8
Fat	4.5g
Cholesterol	0.0mg
Sodium	821.4mg
Carbohydrates	106.4g
Protein	16.9g

* Percent Daily Values are based on a 2,000 calorie diet.

New England Style Stuffed Mushrooms

Ingredients

- 1/4 C. olive oil
- 24 large white mushrooms
- 12 oz. flaked crabmeat
- 4 tbsp chopped onions
- 1 tsp dry mustard
- 1 C. shredded parmesan cheese
- 1 C. soft breadcrumbs
- 2 tsp parsley, chopped
- 1/8 tsp ground red pepper
- 1/8 tsp black pepper
- 1/8 tsp garlic salt
- 1 egg, beaten
- 3 tbsp mayonnaise
- 1/2 C. melted butter
- 1/4 tsp garlic salt
- 2 C. shredded parmesan cheese

Directions

- Before you do anything, preheat the oven to 350 F. Grease a baking dish with some butter. Place it aside.
- Clean the mushrooms, rinse them and dry them. Cut off the mushroom stems and chop them.
- Get a mixing bowl: Place in it the chopped stems with crabmeat, onion, mustard, 1 C. parmesan cheese, soft bread crumbs, parsley, red and black pepper, and 1/8 tsp garlic salt.
- Add the egg with mayo and combine them well to make the filling.
- Place the mushroom caps in the greased dish. Spoon the filling into the mushroom caps.
- Place the small pan over medium heat. Stir in it the butter with 1/4 tsp garlic salt until they melt.
- Drizzle the mixture all over the stuffed mushroom caps. Sprinkle the remaining cheese on top.
- Place the stuffed mushroom dish in the oven. Let it cook for 22 to 26 min. Serve it warm. Enjoy.

Servings per Recipe: 1

Timing Information:

Preparation	30 mins
Total Time	55 mins

Nutritional Information:

Calories	133.9
Fat	10.1g
Cholesterol	34.8mg
Sodium	357.2mg
Carbohydrates	2.4g
Protein	8.6g

* Percent Daily Values are based on a 2,000 calorie diet.

SANDRA'S SALISBURY STEAK

Ingredients

Steak

- 1 lb. ground beef
- 1/3 C. chopped onion
- 1/4 C. cracker crumb
- 1 egg, beaten
- 1 1/2 tbsp horseradish
- 1 tsp salt
- 1 tsp pepper
- 2 tbsp butter
- 1 medium onion, sliced into, rings

- 8 oz. fresh mushrooms, sliced
- 3 tbsp butter

Gravy

- 3 tbsp flour
- salt
- pepper
- 1/2 C. cream
- 3/4 C. chicken broth
- 1 dash Worcestershire sauce
- 1 dash hot sauce

Directions

- Get a mixing bowl: Mix in it the ground beef, chopped onions, cracker crumbs, egg, horseradish, salt and pepper. Form the mixture into 2 burgers. Place a pan over medium heat. Heat in it 2 tbsp of butter until it melts. Add the burgers and let them cook for 9 min on each side.
- Place a small pan over medium heat. Heat in it the remaining butter. Cook in it the onion with mushroom for 6 min. Drain the steak burgers and place them aside. Mix the flour into the juices in the pan with a pinch of salt and pepper. Let them cook for 2 to 3 min while stirring them all the time. Add the cream and stir them until they become thick. Stir in the broth until you get a smooth sauce. Let it cook until it becomes slightly thick.
- Stir in the Worcestershire sauce with hot sauce.
- Stir in the mushroom and onion mix with the steak burgers. Let them cook for 12 min over low heat.Serve your steak burgers with the mushroom gravy warm with some rice.
- Get a mixing bowl: Enjoy.

Servings per Recipe: 2

Timing Information:

Preparation	20 mins
Total Time	1 hr

Nutritional Information:

Calories	1132.2
Fat	85.1g
Cholesterol	44.2g
Sodium	1951.2mg
Carbohydrates	36.4g
Protein	56.1g

* Percent Daily Values are based on a 2,000 calorie diet.

STIR FRIED MUSHROOMS FOR TOPPING

Ingredients

- 1/2 lb. sliced mushrooms
- 1 medium onion, wedges
- 2 tbsp butter
- 1 tbsp olive oil
- 1 tsp Worcestershire sauce
- 1/4 tsp garlic salt

Directions

- Place a pan over medium heat. Heat in it the oil with butter.
- Stir in the onion with mushroom. Let them cook for 22 min until they become soft.
- Stir in the Worcestershire sauce and garlic salt. Serve your stir fry warm with some grilled steaks.
- Enjoy.

Servings per Recipe: 4

Timing Information:

Preparation	10 mins
Total Time	40 mins

Nutritional Information:

Calories	105.9
Fat	9.3g
Cholesterol	15.2mg
Sodium	68.7mg
Carbohydrates	4.8g
Protein	2.1g

* Percent Daily Values are based on a 2,000 calorie diet.

German Egg Noodle and Chuck Dinner

Ingredients

- 7 1/2-8 lbs. boneless beef chuck roast, cut into chunks
- coarse ground black pepper
- oil
- 1 (32 oz.) boxes beef broth
- 1 large onion sectioned and separated
- 1 (1 oz.) envelope French onion soup mix
- 1/4 C. A.1. Original Sauce
- 1 tbsp minced garlic
- 4 tbsp butter
- salt
- 2 (8 oz.) containers sliced mushrooms
- 4 tbsp cornstarch
- 4 tbsp cold water
- 2 (16 oz.) bags frozen egg noodles, cooked and drained

Directions

- Place a large pot over medium heat. Heat in it a splash of oil.
- Cook in it the beef roast for 4 to 6 min on each side. Stir in the broth, onion, soup mix, A-1, garlic, butter and salt.
- Let them cook for 100 min over low heat. Stir in the mushroom and let them cook for an extra 16 to 22 min.
- Once the time is up, remove the cover.
- Get a small mixing bowl: Whisk in it the cornstarch with water. Stir it into the pot.
- Let them cook for 6 min until the sauce becomes slightly thick. Stir in the noodles.
- Adjust the seasoning of your noodles stew then serve it warm.
- Enjoy.

Servings per Recipe: 10

Timing Information:

Preparation	15 mins
Total Time	2 hrs. 15 mins

Nutritional Information:

Calories	911.2
Fat	29.6g
Cholesterol	313.3mg
Sodium	903.8mg
Carbohydrates	74.0g
Protein	87.7g

* Percent Daily Values are based on a 2,000 calorie diet.

Cube Steak Clásico

Ingredients

Steaks

- 4 cube steaks
- 3 -4 tbsp cracked black pepper
- 1 tbsp kosher salt
- 1 tbsp olive oil
- 1 tbsp soft butter

Sauce

- 8 oz. cremini mushrooms, sliced
- 1 shallot, peeled and minced
- 2 garlic cloves, peeled and minced
- 1 tbsp basil, chopped
- 1 C. heavy cream
- 2 tbsp soft unsalted butter

Directions

For the meat:

- Sprinkle some salt and pepper all over the steak cubes.
- Place a pan over medium heat. Heat in it the oil. Cook in it the steak dices for 5 to 7 min while stirring them often.
- Drain them and cover them with a piece of foil.
- heat the rest of the butter in the same pan. Cook in it the mushroom and shallot for 5 min.
- Add the garlic and cook them for 1 min. Stir in the cooked steak dices with cream. Let them cook until the cream reduce by 1/3.
- Adjust the seasoning of your cream steak pan then serve it hot with noodles.
- Enjoy.

Servings per Recipe: 4

Timing Information:

| Preparation | 15 mins |
| Total Time | 30 mins |

Nutritional Information:

Calories	342.9
Fat	34.2g
Cholesterol	104.4mg
Sodium	1798.2mg
Carbohydrates	8.7g
Protein	3.5g

* Percent Daily Values are based on a 2,000 calorie diet.

Dijon Chicken

Ingredients

- 4 boneless skinless chicken breast halves
- 2 tbsp flour
- 2 tbsp vegetable oil
- 1 tbsp butter
- 1 small onion, chopped
- 1 C. mushroom, sliced
- 1/2 C. light cream
- 1 tbsp fresh parsley, chopped
- 1 tbsp Dijon mustard
- 1 tbsp lemon juice

Directions

- Place the chicken breasts between 2 wax sheets. Use a kitchen hammer or pan to flatten them until they become 1/4 inch thick.
- Season the chicken breasts with some salt and pepper. Dust them with flour.
- Place a pan over medium heat. Heat in it the oil. Cook in it the chicken breasts for 7 to 9 min on each side.
- Drain the chicken breasts and place them aside.
- Heat the butter in the pan over high heat. Cook in it the mushroom with onion for 6 min.
- Lower the heat. Stir in the cream with parsley, mustard and lemon juice.
- Let them cook until they start boiling while stirring them often.
- Transfer the chicken breasts into serving plates. Drizzle the mushroom sauce over then serve them hot.
- Enjoy.

Servings per Recipe: 4

Timing Information:

Preparation	15 mins
Total Time	30 mins

Nutritional Information:

Calories	307.3
Fat	18.8g
Cholesterol	102.9mg
Sodium	219.0mg
Carbohydrates	6.8g
Protein	27.2g

* Percent Daily Values are based on a 2,000 calorie diet.

CREAMY PORTABELLA SOUP

Ingredients

- 4 tbsp unsalted butter
- 2 leeks, halved lengthwise and sliced
- 1 large onion, chopped
- 3 large portabella mushrooms, dark gills scraped out, chopped
- 3 tbsp all-purpose flour
- 1 1/2 tsp dried thyme leaves
- 1 bay leaf
- 6 C. low sodium chicken broth
- 1 tsp salt
- 1 tsp sugar
- 1/2 tsp pepper
- 1 C. heavy cream
- 1/4 C. chopped parsley

Directions

- Place a large pot over medium heat. Heat in it the butter. Cook in it the leeks with onion for 4 min.
- Stir in the mushroom and let them cook for 11 min over low heat with the lid on.
- Add the flour and cook them for 2 min over medium heat. Stir in the thyme, bay leaf, broth, salt, sugar, and pepper.
- Put on half a cover then let them cook for 12 min.
- Allow the soup to sit for few minutes. Discard the bay lead then use an immersion blender to blend it smooth.
- Stir the cream into the soup with a pinch of salt and pepper. Heat it for few minutes then serve it warm.
- Enjoy.

Servings per Recipe: 8

Timing Information:

Preparation	10 mins
Total Time	45 mins

Nutritional Information:

Calories	223.8
Fat	18.0g
Cholesterol	56.0mg
Sodium	365.9mg
Carbohydrates	12.0g
Protein	5.8g

* Percent Daily Values are based on a 2,000 calorie diet.

CHICKEN WITH MUSHROOM AND THYME SAUCE

Ingredients

- 1/3 C. all-purpose flour
- 1 1/2 tsp dried thyme
- 1/2 tsp ground allspice
- 4 large boneless skinless chicken breast halves
- 1/4 C. butter
- 1 lb. mushroom, sliced
- 1 small onion, chopped
- 1 C. whipping cream
- 1 C. canned low sodium chicken broth

Directions

- Before you do anything, preheat the oven to 350 F.
- Get a mixing bowl: Combine in it the flour, 1/2 tsp thyme and allspice. Reserve 1 tbsp of it aside.
- Season the chicken breasts with some salt and pepper. Dust them with the flour mix.
- Place a pan over medium heat. Heat in it the butter. Cook in it the chicken over medium heat for 4 to 6 min on each side.
- Once the time is up, drain the chicken breasts and place them aside.
- Stir the mushrooms, onion, and remaining 1 tsp thyme into the same pan.
- Let them cook for 6 min. Stir in the remaining 1 tbsp of the flour mix you put aside. Stir them for 1 min.
- Stir into the broth with cream. Let them cook until they start boiling.
- Stir the cooked chicken breasts back into the pan. Heat them for 6 min. Serve your creamy chicken and mushroom warm with some noodles or rice.
- Enjoy.

Servings per Recipe: 4

Timing Information:

Preparation	5 mins
Total Time	20 mins

Nutritional Information:

Calories	523.1
Fat	37.5g
Cholesterol	187.5mg
Sodium	285.8mg
Carbohydrates	16.1g
Protein	32.4g

* Percent Daily Values are based on a 2,000 calorie diet.

Mushroom Lasagna

Ingredients

- 9 -10 lasagna noodles, uncooked
- 1 (14 oz.) cans diced tomatoes with juice, undrained
- 1 (8 oz.) cans tomato sauce
- 1 (6 oz.) cans tomato paste
- 1 tbsp balsamic vinegar
- 1 tbsp dried basil
- 1 tsp dried oregano
- 1/2-1 tsp garlic powder
- salt and pepper
- 2 C. shredded mozzarella cheese, divided
- 1 C. feta cheese, crumbled
- 1 (10 oz.) packages frozen chopped spinach, thawed and squeezed dry
- 1 egg, slightly beaten
- 1/2-1 lb. portabella mushroom, sliced

Directions

- Before you do anything, preheat the oven to 350 F. Grease a casserole dish.
- Prepare the noodles by following the instructions on the package.
- Place a saucepan over medium heat. Combine in it the tomatoes (with juice), tomato sauce, tomato paste, vinegar and seasonings.
- Bring them to a boil. Lower the heat and put on the lid. Let them cook for 22 to 26 min.
- Pour 1/3 of the sauce into the greased pan and spread it in an even layer.
- Cover it with 3 noodles sheets. Spread over them 1/2 of the cheese mix, 1/2 of the mushroom slices and 1/3 of the tomato sauce.
- Repeat the process to make another layer ending with noodles and tomato sauce on top.
- Sprinkle the mozzarella cheese over it. Lay a loose sheet of foil over the dish. Place the lasagna in the oven and let it cook for 26 min.
- Once the time is up, discard the foil and cook it for an extra 5 min. Serve it warm
- Get a mixing bowl: Enjoy.

Servings per Recipe: 8

Timing Information:

| Preparation | 40 mins |
| Total Time | 1 hr 10 mins |

Nutritional Information:

Calories	288.5
Fat	11.7g
Cholesterol	62.0mg
Sodium	814.3mg
Carbohydrates	31.1g
Protein	16.6g

* Percent Daily Values are based on a 2,000 calorie diet.

CENTRAL EUROPEAN STYLE MUSHROOM SOUP

Ingredients

- 12 oz. mushrooms, -sliced
- 2 C. onions, chopped
- 2 tbsp butter
- 3 tbsp flour
- 1 C. milk
- 2 tsp dill weed
- 1 tbsp Hungarian paprika
- 1 tbsp tamari soy sauce
- 1 tsp salt
- 2 C. stock
- 2 tsp lemon juice
- 1/4 C. parsley, chopped
- ground black pepper, -
- 1/2 C. sour cream

Directions

- Place a soup pot over medium heat. Stir in it 2 tbsp of stock with onion and a pinch of salt.
- Let them cook for 3 min. Stir in the mushroom with 1 tsp dill, 1/2 C. stock or water, soy sauce, and paprika.
- Put on the lid and let them cook for 16 min over low heat.
- Place a heavy saucepan over medium heat. Heat in it the butter until it melts.
- Mix into it the flour and cook it for 2 min. Stir in the milk and whisk them until they become smooth for 11 min
- Stir it into the soup pot with the rest of the stock. Put on the lid and let them cook for 12 to 16 min.
- Stir in the lemon juice, sour cream and parsley.
- Adjust the seasoning of your soup then serve it warm with your favorite toppings.
- Enjoy.

Servings per Recipe: 4

Timing Information:

Preparation	20 mins
Total Time	45 mins

Nutritional Information:

Calories	226.9
Fat	14.3g
Cholesterol	38.7mg
Sodium	947.2mg
Carbohydrates	19.9g
Protein	7.6g

* Percent Daily Values are based on a 2,000 calorie diet.

MONDAY'S MUSHROOM STIR FRY

Ingredients

- 1 lb. asparagus spear, trimmed
- 1/4 C. butter
- 2 C. mushrooms, sliced
- 2 tbsp Dijon mustard
- 1/4 tsp ground black pepper
- 1/2 tsp garlic, minced
- salt

Directions

- Place a pan over medium heat. Lay in it the asparagus and cover it with water.
- Bring them to a rolling boil for 6 to 8 min until they become tender.
- Discard the water from the pan. Stir the rest of the ingredients into the asparagus.
- Let them cook for 6 min. serve it warm.
- Enjoy.

Servings per Recipe: 4

Timing Information:

Preparation	10 mins
Total Time	25 mins

Nutritional Information:

Calories	140.2
Fat	12.1g
Cholesterol	30.5mg
Sodium	183.4mg
Carbohydrates	6.6g
Protein	4.2g

* Percent Daily Values are based on a 2,000 calorie diet.

VERMONT SOUP

Ingredients

- 6 tbsp butter
- 2 C. -minced yellow onions
- 1/2 tsp sugar
- 1 lb. fresh mushrooms
- 1/4 C. flour
- 1 C. water
- 1 3/4 C. chicken broth
- 1 C. dry vermouth
- 1 tsp salt
- 1/2 tsp pepper
- 1 tsp thyme

Directions

- Place a saucepan over medium heat. Heat in it the butter. Stir in the onions, sugar, and thyme. Let them cook for 35 min over low heat.
- Stir in the mushroom and let them cook for 6 min.
- Add the flour and mi them well. Let them cook for 3 min while always stirring them.
- Stir in the remaining ingredients. Bring them to a boil. Lower the heat and let them cook for 14 min over low heat.
- Adjust the seasoning of your soup then serve it warm.
- Enjoy.

Servings per Recipe: 4

Timing Information:

Preparation	20 mins
Total Time	1 hr 50 mins

Nutritional Information:

Calories	307.0
Fat	18.4g
Cholesterol	45.8mg
Sodium	1073.9mg
Carbohydrates	19.9g
Protein	7.6g

* Percent Daily Values are based on a 2,000 calorie diet.

GARDEN PARTY MUSHROOM GRILLER

Ingredients

- 1/2 lb. whole mushrooms
- 1/4 C. margarine, melted
- 1/2 tsp dill weed
- 1/2 tsp garlic salt

Directions

- Before you do anything, preheat the grill and grease it.
- Get a mixing bowl: Mix in it the margarine, dill, and garlic salt.
- Stick the mushroom into skewers. Coat them with the margarine mix.
- Place the mushroom skewers on the grill. Cook them for 5 to 6 min.
- Serve them warm with some sour cream.
- Enjoy.

Servings per Recipe: 4

Timing Information:

Preparation	10 mins
Total Time	25 mins

Nutritional Information:

Calories	64.5
Fat	5.8g
Cholesterol	0.0mg
Sodium	69.6mg
Carbohydrates	2.2g
Protein	1.8g

* Percent Daily Values are based on a 2,000 calorie diet.

Parmesan Stuffed Mushroom Bites

Ingredients

- 24 large mushrooms, stems removed and stems chopped
- 2 tbsp butter
- 1 C. onion, diced
- 1/4 tsp dried thyme
- 1 1/2 C. spinach, chopped
- 3 tbsp breadcrumbs
- 1/2 C. parmesan cheese, grated
- salt and pepper

Directions

- Before you do anything, preheat the oven to 350 F. Coat a baking sheet with 1 tbsp of butter.
- Place a pan over medium heat. Heat in it the butter until it melts.
- Cook in it the thyme with onion for 3 min.. Stir in the mushroom stems with spinach and breadcrumbs.
- Let them cook for 6 min over high heat. Turn off the heat then stir it the parmesan cheese with a pinch of salt and pepper.
- Place the mushroom caps on the greased sheet. Spoon the filling into them.
- Dot them with the remaining butter. Place the sheet in the oven and let them cook for 16 to 21 min.
- Serve your stuffed mushroom caps warm.
- Enjoy.

Servings per Recipe: 6

Timing Information:

Preparation	15 mins
Total Time	45 mins

Nutritional Information:

Calories	209.3
Fat	8.0g
Cholesterol	17.5mg
Sodium	370.4mg
Carbohydrates	25.5g
Protein	10.2g

* Percent Daily Values are based on a 2,000 calorie diet.

BELLA BURGERS

Ingredients

- 4 large portabella mushrooms
- 1/4 C. balsamic vinegar
- 2 tbsp olive oil
- 1 tsp dried basil
- 1 tsp dried oregano
- 2 -4 cloves garlic, minced
- salt and pepper
- 4 oz. sliced provolone cheese
- 4 whole wheat rolls
- sliced tomatoes
- romaine lettuce leaf
- sliced grilled onion
- Dijon mustard

Directions

- Cut off the mushroom stems and discard them.
- Lay the mushroom caps on a lined up baking sheet with the smooth side facing up.
- Season them with some salt and pepper.
- Get a mixing bowl: Mix in it the vinegar, oil, basil, oregano, and garlic to make the marinade.
- Drizzle it all over the mushroom caps. Let them sit for 12 to 16 min.
- Before you do anything, preheat the grill and grease it.
- Drain the mushroom caps and reserve the marinade. Place them over the grill.
- Let the mushroom cook for 3 to 4 min on each side. Baste them with the reserved marinade every once in a while.
- Lay on them the cheese slices and cook them for an extra minute.
- Place the cheesy mushroom in a bread rolls with your favorite toppings and sauce.
- Enjoy.

Servings per Recipe: 4

Timing Information:

Preparation	15 mins
Total Time	35 mins

Nutritional Information:

Calories	554.2
Fat	20.9g
Cholesterol	19.6mg
Sodium	801.9mg
Carbohydrates	76.3g
Protein	21.0g

* Percent Daily Values are based on a 2,000 calorie diet.

EASY CHICKEN MARSALA

Ingredients

- 1 lb. boneless skinless chicken breast
- kosher salt
- pepper
- 3 tbsp olive oil
- 6 oz. cremini mushrooms, sliced
- 2 garlic cloves, minced
- 1/2 C. dry marsala
- 1/3 C. heavy cream
- 2 oz. crumbled gorgonzola
- 2 tbsp chopped Italian parsley

Directions

- Cut the chicken breast into 3/4 inch slices. Sprinkle over them some salt and pepper.
- Place a pan over medium heat. Heat in it 2 tbsp of oil. Cook in it half of the chicken slices for 2 to 3 min on each side.
- Drain them and place them aside. Repeat the process with the remaining chicken slices.
- Heat 1 tbsp of oil in the same pan. Cook in it the mushroom with a pinch of salt for 4 min.
- Stir in the garlic and cook them for 1 min. Stir in the marsala and let them cook for 2 to 3 min.
- Add the cream and cook them for 2 min. Stir in 2/3 of the gorgonzola cheese. Stir them until they melt.
- Adjust the seasoning of the sauce. Stir in the cooked chicken stripes and heat them for few minutes.
- Garnish your creamy chicken and mushroom skillet with some parsley, and the remaining cheese.
- Enjoy.

Servings per Recipe: 2

Timing Information:

Preparation	20 mins
Total Time	40 mins

Nutritional Information:

Calories	739.6
Fat	46.0g
Cholesterol	207.2mg
Sodium	569.1mg
Carbohydrates	8.1g
Protein	61.7g

* Percent Daily Values are based on a 2,000 calorie diet.

ALTERNATIVE GRATIN

Ingredients

- 1/4 C. butter
- 2 lbs. mushrooms, sliced
- 3 garlic cloves, minced
- 2/3 C. sour cream
- salt and pepper
- 2 tbsp all-purpose flour
- 1/4 C. chopped parsley
- 1 C. shredded mozzarella cheese

Directions

- Before you do anything, preheat the oven to 400 F. Coat a casserole dish with a cooking spray.
- Place a pan over medium heat. Heat in it the butter. Cook in it the mushroom for 4 min.
- Add the garlic and cook them for 1 min.
- Get a mixing bowl: Mix in it the sour cream with flour, a pinch of salt and pepper.
- Stir it into the mushroom. Cook them until they start boiling.
- Spoon the mixture into the greased dish. Top it with shredded mozzarella and parsley.
- Place the casserole in the oven and let it cook for 12 to 16 min.
- Serve it warm with some rice or noodles.
- Enjoy.

Servings per Recipe: 4

Timing Information:

| Preparation | 10 mins |
| Total Time | 20 mins |

Nutritional Information:

Calories	328.1
Fat	26.1g
Cholesterol	72.5mg
Sodium	321.4mg
Carbohydrates	12.9g
Protein	14.7g

* Percent Daily Values are based on a 2,000 calorie diet.

6-Ingredient Mushrooms Greek Style

Ingredients

- 1/4 C. olive oil
- 1 lb. white mushroom, halved
- 3 tbsp balsamic vinegar
- 1 tsp salt
- 1/4 tsp red pepper flakes
- pepper

Directions

- Place a pan over medium heat. Heat in it the oil. Cook in it the mushroom for 5 to 6 min.
- Add the vinegar, red pepper flakes salt and a pinch of pepper. Let them cook for 1 min.
- Serve your mushroom warm with as a side dish or a sandwich topping.
- Enjoy.

Servings per Recipe: 4

Timing Information:

Preparation	2 mins
Total Time	9 mins

Nutritional Information:

Calories	155.2
Fat	13.9g
Cholesterol	0.0mg
Sodium	590.1mg
Carbohydrates	5.8g
Protein	3.5g

* Percent Daily Values are based on a 2,000 calorie diet.

SEATTLE STYLE ASPARAGUS SKILLET

Ingredients

- 1/2 small onion, sliced
- 1 1/2 C. mushrooms, sliced
- 1 1/2 C. asparagus, chopped tips and most tender parts
- 3 -4 tbsp butter
- salt and pepper

Directions

- Place a pan over medium heat. Heat in it the butter. Sauté in it the onion for 3 min.
- Stir in the mushroom and let it cook for 3 min. Stir in the asparagus with a pinch of salt and pepper.
- Let them cook for 3 to 4 min. Serve it warm.
- Enjoy.

Servings per Recipe: 2

Timing Information:

Preparation	10 mins
Total Time	20 mins

Nutritional Information:

Calories	200.9
Fat	17.7g
Cholesterol	45.8mg
Sodium	174.3mg
Carbohydrates	8.9g
Protein	5.2g

* Percent Daily Values are based on a 2,000 calorie diet.

ROASTED VEGETABLE SAMPLER

Ingredients

- 3 medium zucchini, halved lengthwise and sliced
- 1 1/2 C. sliced mushrooms
- 1 yellow onion, sliced and separated into rings
- 2 -3 tsp extra virgin olive oil
- 1/4 tsp salt
- 1/2 tsp dried Italian seasoning

Directions

- Before you do anything, preheat the oven to 450 F.
- Get a mixing bowl: Stir in it all the ingredients.
- Transfer them to a roasting tray and spray in an even layer.
- Place it in the oven and let them cook for 16 min.
- Toss the veggies and let them cook for an extra 8 min. Serve them warm.
- Enjoy.

Servings per Recipe: 4

Timing Information:

Preparation	5 mins
Total Time	30 mins

Nutritional Information:

Calories	61.6
Fat	2.8g
Cholesterol	0.0mg
Sodium	159.5mg
Carbohydrates	8.0g
Protein	2.8g

* Percent Daily Values are based on a 2,000 calorie diet.

HANDMADE STUFFING

Ingredients

- 1/2 C. uncooked wild rice
- 4 C. cubed day-old French bread
- 1/2 C. butter
- 1 large onion, chopped
- 1 garlic clove, minced
- 3 C. fresh mushrooms, sliced
- 1/2 tsp sage
- 1/2 tsp dried thyme leaves, crushed
- 1/2 tsp salt
- 1/4 tsp black pepper
- 1 C. chicken broth, from giblet boil
- 1/2 C. chopped pecans

Directions

- Prepare the rice by following the instructions on the package.
- Before you do anything, preheat the oven to 350 F.
- Lay the bread cubes on a lined up baking sheet. Place it 5 inches away from the heat source.
- Let them cook for 2 min. Place them aside to cool down.
- Place a pan over medium heat. Heat in it the butter. Cook in it the garlic with onion for 4 min.
- Stir in the mushroom and cook them for another 4 min. Stir in the sage with thyme, a pinch of salt and pepper.
- Let them cook for 1 min. Add the broth with pecans and bread cubes.
- Transfer the mixture to a greased casserole dish. Cover it with piece of foil.
- Place it in the oven and let it cook for 42 min.
- Serve your stuffing warm with some turkey or chicken roast.
- Enjoy.

Servings per Recipe: 6

Timing Information:

Preparation	30 mins
Total Time	1 hr 30 mins

Nutritional Information:

Calories	271.4
Fat	22.4g
Cholesterol	40.6mg
Sodium	457.0mg
Carbohydrates	15.1g
Protein	5.1g

* Percent Daily Values are based on a 2,000 calorie diet.

TENNESSEE STYLE CHICKEN BREAST

Ingredients

- 4 large boneless skinless chicken breasts
- 1/4 C. flour
- 3 tbsp butter
- 1 C. mushroom, sliced
- 1/2 C. chicken broth
- 1/4 tsp salt
- 1/8 tsp pepper
- 1/3 C. mozzarella cheese
- 1/3 C. parmesan cheese
- 1/4 C. green onion, sliced

Directions

- Season the chicken breasts with some salt and pepper. Dust them with flour.
- Before you do anything, preheat the oven to 350 F.
- Place a pan over medium heat. Heat in it the butter. Cook in it the chicken breasts for 3 to 5 min on each side.
- Drain them and place them on a baking sheet.
- Cook the mushroom in the same pan for 3 min. Stir in the broth with a pinch of salt and pepper.
- Cook them until they start boiling. Keep them cooking for 6 min.
- Pour the mushroom mixture over the chicken breasts. Place them in the oven and let them cook for 16 min.
- Once the time is up, top them with cheese and green onions.
- Cook them for an extra 6 min in the oven. Serve them warm.
- Enjoy.

Servings per Recipe: 4

Timing Information:

Preparation	15 mins
Total Time	42 mins

Nutritional Information:

Calories	314.0
Fat	16.4g
Cholesterol	113.1mg
Sodium	639.3mg
Carbohydrates	7.7g
Protein	32.5g

* Percent Daily Values are based on a 2,000 calorie diet.

30-Minute Mushroom Rotini

Ingredients

- 12 oz. rotini noodles
- 1 tbsp olive oil
- 3 cloves garlic, minced
- 1 C. onion, chopped
- 1 tbsp thyme
- 4 C. mixed mushrooms, sliced
- 2 tbsp all-purpose flour
- 2 C. milk
- 2 C. spinach, rinsed well & chopped
- 1/2 C. basil, chopped
- 1 tsp salt
- ground pepper
- grated parmesan cheese

Directions

- Place a skillet over medium heat. Heat in it the oil. Sauté in it the thyme with onion and garlic for 2 min.
- Stir in the mushroom and cook them for 7 to 9 min.
- Add the flour and mix them for 1 min while cooking. Stir in the milk gradually.
- Let them cook until they start boiling. Let them cook for 3 min stirring them all the time until they become thick.
- Add the spinach with basil, a pinch of salt and pepper. Cook them for 4 min.
- Serve your creamy mushroom and spinach skillet with some noodles.
- Enjoy.

Servings per Recipe: 4

Timing Information:

Preparation	15 mins
Total Time	30 mins

Nutritional Information:

Calories	477.1
Fat	9.5g
Cholesterol	17.0mg
Sodium	664.0mg
Carbohydrates	79.6g
Protein	18.8g

* Percent Daily Values are based on a 2,000 calorie diet.

Italian Seasoned Buttons

Ingredients

- 3 oz. butter
- 2 garlic cloves, crushed
- 13 oz. button mushrooms, wiped clean
- salt
- black pepper
- 1/4 tsp cayenne pepper
- 2 tbsp parsley, chopped
- 1 tbsp basil, chopped
- bread, assorted crusty

Directions

- Place a pan over medium heat. Heat in it the butter. Sauté in it the garlic for 1 min.
- Stir in the mushroom. Cook them for 5 min over high heat.
- Stir in the cayenne, parsley, basil, a pinch of salt and pepper. Let them cook for 2 min.
- Serve your herbed mushroom skillet warm as a side dish or a topping.
- Enjoy.

Servings per Recipe: 4

Timing Information:

Preparation	15 mins
Total Time	30 mins

Nutritional Information:

Calories	151.5
Fat	15.3g
Cholesterol	40.0mg
Sodium	137.7mg
Carbohydrates	2.8g
Protein	2.3g

* Percent Daily Values are based on a 2,000 calorie diet.

ALASKAN TROUT DINNER

Ingredients

- 5 (3/4 lb.) trout, cleaned and dried
- 1/2 C. olive oil
- 5 cloves garlic, chopped
- ground black pepper
- salt
- 1/2-3/4 lb. mushrooms
- 1/4-1/2 C. butter
- 4 tbsp fine dry breadcrumbs
- 4 green onions, sliced
- 3 fresh lemons
- 2 tbsp minced parsley

Directions

- Before you do anything, preheat the oven to 350 F.
- Brush the whole trout with some olive oil. Season it with some salt and pepper.
- Lay half of the mushroom slices in the bottom of a casserole dish. Top it with the trout fish.
- Sprinkle the bread crumbs over it followed by the parsley garlic and green onion.
- Play a small pan over medium heat. Heat in it the butter with olive oil and the juice of 2 lemons.
- Drizzle the mixture over the trout fish. Place it in the oven and let it cook for 22 to 26 min.
- Place a skillet over medium heat. Heat in it some butter. Cook in it the remaining mushroom for 3min.
- Lay it over the baked trout fish then serve it warm with some rice.
- Enjoy.

Servings per Recipe: 5

Timing Information:

Preparation	5 mins
Total Time	32 mins

Nutritional Information:

Calories	825.8
Fat	53.8g
Cholesterol	221.6mg
Sodium	304.0mg
Carbohydrates	10.5g
Protein	73.6g

* Percent Daily Values are based on a 2,000 calorie diet.

GRILLED MUSHROOM PARCEL

Ingredients

- 1 lemon
- 1 tbsp dried parsley
- 1/2 tbsp olive oil
- 3 garlic cloves, minced
- 2 green onions, chopped
- 1 lb. mushroom, cleaned
- salt and pepper,

Directions

- Before you do anything, preheat the grill and grease it.
- Place the mushroom in a large piece of oil. Crumble the sides to prevent the juices from spilling.
- Add to it the lemon juice and zest with the remaining ingredients. Toss them to coat.
- Place the mushroom parcel over the grill. Let it cook for 7 to 8 min.
- Serve it warm as a side dish or topping.
- Enjoy.

Servings per Recipe: 4

Timing Information:

Preparation	15 mins
Total Time	15 mins

Nutritional Information:

Calories	51.0
Fat	2.1g
Cholesterol	0.0mg
Sodium	9.4mg
Carbohydrates	6.5g
Protein	4.0g

* Percent Daily Values are based on a 2,000 calorie diet.

BELL MUSHROOM STEAK SANDWICH

Ingredients

- 2 onions, sliced
- 2 tbsp butter
- 2 tbsp oil
- 1 lb. white button mushrooms, sliced
- 2 tbsp minced garlic
- 1 C. beef broth
- 3 tbsp whipping cream
- 3 tbsp ketchup
- 1 tbsp Worcestershire sauce
- 2 tsp Dijon mustard
- 1 lb. cooked leftover steak
- salt and pepper
- 1 large green bell pepper, seeded and sliced
- sliced mozzarella cheese
- 1 loaf unsliced bread halved lengthwise

Directions

- Before you do anything, preheat the oven broiler.
- Coat each bread half with butter. Broil the bread for 2 to 4 min until it becomes crisp. Place a pan over medium heat. Heat in it the oil. Cook in it the onion with a pinch of salt and pepper for 4 min
- Stir in mushroom with garlic. Cook them for 4 min. Add more butter or oil if needed. Drain the mushroom mix and place it aside. Stir the beef broth with Worcestershire sauce and black pepper into the same pan. Heat them for 3 min. Stir in the whipping cream, ketchup and mustard. Let them cook for another 3 min over low heat. Stir in the mushroom mixture with beef slices. Let them cook for 4 min over low heat. Lay the bottom half of the bread on a large plate. Lay over it some cheese slices.
- Top it with the steak and mushroom mixture. Lay over it the bell pepper slices, followed some extra cheese slices.
- Cover them with the top bread half. Slice the sandwich into serving slices then serve them right away. Enjoy.

Servings per Recipe: 4

Timing Information:

| Preparation | 45 mins |
| Total Time | 45 mins |

Nutritional Information:

Calories	699.1
Fat	27.4g
Cholesterol	120.2mg
Sodium	1063.5mg
Carbohydrates	66.8g
Protein	47.0g 94

* Percent Daily Values are based on a 2,000 calorie diet.

CHINESE MUSHROOM SAUCEPAN

Ingredients

- 1/8 C. extra virgin olive oil
- 1/8 C. sesame oil
- 1/4 C. white vinegar
- 2 tbsp soy sauce
- 2 tbsp chopped garlic
- 5 C. mushrooms
- 2 tbsp sliced green onions

Directions

- Place a heavy saucepan over medium heat. Stir in it the oil, vinegar, soy sauce, garlic and mushrooms.
- Cook them until they start boiling. Lower the heat and let them cook for an extra 16 min.
- Drain the mushrooms and transfer them to a serving plate.
- Garnish them with green onions then serve it warm.
- Enjoy.

Servings per Recipe: 8

Timing Information:

Preparation	5 mins
Total Time	25 mins

Nutritional Information:

Calories	77.4
Fat	6.9g
Cholesterol	0.0mg
Sodium	254.5mg
Carbohydrates	2.5g
Protein	1.9g

* Percent Daily Values are based on a 2,000 calorie diet.

FULL VEGETARIAN STROGANOFF

Ingredients

- 1 (6 C.) packages pasta, egg-free ribbon noodles
- 1/4 C. margarine, vegan
- 1 onion, minced
- 16 oz. portabella mushrooms, sliced
- 2 garlic cloves, minced
- 2 C. vegetable broth, beef flavored
- 1 tsp salt
- 1 tsp black pepper
- 1 tbsp Worcestershire sauce, vegan
- 1/4 C. flour
- 1 C. vegan sour cream

Directions

- Prepare the noodles by following the instructions on the package.
- Place a pan over medium heat. Heat in it the margarine. Cook in it the onion with mushroom for 5 min.
- Stir in the garlic and cook them for 1 min.
- Place a saucepan over medium heat. Heat in it the broth until it starts boiling.
- Stir in the salt, pepper and Worcestershire sauce. Add the flour and mix them well.
- Let them cook until the sauce become thick. Add the sauce to the mushroom skillet.
- Add the sour cream and stir them well. Serve your creamy mushroom right away with noodles.
- Enjoy.

Servings per Recipe: 6

Timing Information:

Preparation	10 mins
Total Time	30 mins

Nutritional Information:

Calories	460.2
Fat	9.3g
Cholesterol	0.0mg
Sodium	517.4mg
Carbohydrates	79.2g
Protein	14.6g

* Percent Daily Values are based on a 2,000 calorie diet.

Tuesday's Dinner

(Herbed Mushroom Chicken with Rice)

Ingredients

- 1 tbsp olive oil
- 6 chicken thighs
- 1/2 tsp salt
- 1/2 tsp black pepper
- 2 tbsp butter
- 16 oz. button mushrooms, sliced
- 1 C. yellow onion, sliced
- 1 tbsp garlic, minced
- 2 tbsp all-purpose flour
- 2 tbsp tomato paste
- 2 C. dark chicken stock
- 2 tbsp rosemary leaves, chopped

- 4 C. steamed cooked white rice
- 2 tbsp parsley leaves, chopped

Country Spice Mix

- 2 1/2 tbsp paprika
- 2 tbsp salt
- 2 tbsp garlic powder
- 1 tbsp black pepper
- 1 tbsp onion powder
- 1 tbsp cayenne pepper
- 1 tbsp dried oregano
- 1 tbsp dried thyme

Directions

- Rub the chicken thighs with the spice mix, some salt and pepper.
- Place a skillet over medium heat. Heat in it the oil. Cook in it the chicken thighs for 4 to 5 min on each side.
- Drain them and place them aside. Heat the butter in the same pan. Cook in it the mushroom for 5 min.
- Stir in the onion with garlic. Cook them for 4 min. Add the flour and cook them for another 4 min while stirring them all the time.

- Stir in the tomato paste with stock and rosemary. Let them cook until they start boiling.
- Stir in the chicken back lower the heat. Let them cook for 35 min.
- Once the time is up, flip the chicken thighs and cook them for an extra 35 min.
- Serve your chicken and mushroom skillet warm with some rice.
- Enjoy.

Servings per Recipe: 4

Timing Information:

Preparation	10 mins
Total Time	1 hr 10 mins

Nutritional Information:

Calories	779.0
Fat	34.0g
Cholesterol	137.3mg
Sodium	4189.8mg
Carbohydrates	80.8g
Protein	39.0g

* Percent Daily Values are based on a 2,000 calorie diet.

PARMESAN MUSHROOM BREAKFAST

Ingredients

- 2 tbsp butter
- 3 cloves garlic, minced
- 1/2 C. onion, sliced
- 8 oz. mushrooms, quartered
- 2 C. spinach, chopped
- 6 eggs
- 1/2 tsp salt
- 1 dash pepper
- 1/2 C. grated parmesan cheese

Directions

- Before you do anything, preheat the oven broiler.
- Place an ovenproof pan over medium heat. Heat in it the butter.
- Cook in it the garlic with mushroom and onion for 5 min. Stir in the spinach and cook them for 3 min.
- Get a mixing bowl: Whisk in it the eggs with a pinch of salt and pepper.
- Add it to the mushroom mixture an swirl the pan to make it into an even layer.
- Let it cook for 5 min over low heat until it starts to sit.
- Top the mushroom tart with cheese. Place it in the oven and let it cook for 4 to 5 min.
- Serve your breakfast mushroom tart warm.
- Enjoy.

Servings per Recipe: 2

Timing Information:

Preparation	5 mins
Total Time	20 mins

Nutritional Information:

Calories	478.7
Fat	33.5g
Cholesterol	610.5mg
Sodium	1309.7mg
Carbohydrates	12.1g
Protein	33.6g

* Percent Daily Values are based on a 2,000 calorie diet.

Florida Style Stuffed Mushroom with Shrimp Cream

Ingredients

- 40 medium mushroom caps, cleaned and drained
- 1/3 C. light cream cheese
- 1/4 C. low-fat milk
- 1 clove garlic, minced
- 1 pinch nutmeg
- 1 pinch pepper
- 1/2 tbsp flour
- 1 tbsp low-fat mayonnaise
- 1 tbsp lemon juice
- 3 tbsp parmesan cheese, Kraft
- 1 green onion, sliced thin
- 1 can crabmeat, drained
- 1 can baby shrimp, drained
- 1/2 C. light cheddar cheese, grated
- extra parmesan cheese

Directions

- Before you do anything, preheat the oven to 400 F.
- Place a saucepan over medium heat. Mix in it the flour, cream cheese, milk, garlic, salt, nutmeg, pepper and salt until they melt.
- Mix in the mayonnaise, lemon juice, parmesan cheese and green onion.
- Turn off the heat then stir in the shrimp with crab meat. Put on the lid and let the filling cool down completely.
- Place the mushroom caps in a greased casserole dish. Spoon the filling into them.
- Place the casserole in the oven and let it cook for 16 to 22 min. Serve it warm.
- Enjoy.

Servings per Recipe: 10

Timing Information:

Preparation	30 mins
Total Time	45 mins

Nutritional Information:

Calories	58.2
Fat	2.9g
Cholesterol	8.6mg
Sodium	95.2mg
Carbohydrates	3.7g
Protein	5.4g

* Percent Daily Values are based on a 2,000 calorie diet.

HERBED SAUTÉED MUSHROOM CAPS

Ingredients

- 1 lb. mushroom cap, stemmed and cleaned
- 3 tbsp olive oil
- 1/2 tsp salt
- 1/2 tsp paprika
- 1 garlic clove, crushed
- 1 green onion, chopped
- 3 tbsp fresh parsley, chopped
- 1 tbsp fresh dill weed, chopped
- 2 tsp basil

Directions

- Place a pan over medium heat. Heat in it the oil. Cook in it the green onion with garlic, paprika and salt for 3 min.
- Stir in the mushroom then cook for 6 min. Turn off the heat. Stir in the parsley with basil and dill.
- Adjust the seasoning of your mushroom skillet then serve it warm with some sour cream.
- Enjoy.

Servings per Recipe: 8

Timing Information:

Preparation	10 mins
Total Time	15 mins

Nutritional Information:

Calories	59.3
Fat	5.2g
Cholesterol	0.0mg
Sodium	149.5mg
Carbohydrates	2.2g
Protein	1.8g

* Percent Daily Values are based on a 2,000 calorie diet.

ASIAN-FUSION GINGER MUSHROOM

Ingredients

- 2 tbsp peanut oil
- 1 1/2 lbs. white button mushrooms, cleaned quartered
- 1 tbsp sesame seeds, toasted
- 1 tbsp fresh ginger, minced
- 2 tbsp rice wine vinegar
- 1 tsp sugar
- 2 tbsp soy sauce
- 1 tsp toasted sesame oil
- 2 scallions, sliced

Directions

- Place a pan over medium heat. Heat in it 1 tbsp of peanut oil. Cook in it the mushroom for 6 min.
- Turn the heat to high and let it cook for 7 min. Stir in the remaining peanut oil.
- Lower the heat and let them cook for an extra 8 min. Stir in the ginger with sesame seeds. Let them cook for 40 sec.
- Stir in the rice vinegar, sugar and soy sauce. let them cook for 1 min while stirring them all the time.
- Turn off the heat. Stir in the sesame oil. Garnish it with scallions then serve it warm with some sour cream.
- Enjoy.

Servings per Recipe: 4

Timing Information:

Preparation	10 mins
Total Time	35 mins

Nutritional Information:

Calories	133.0
Fat	9.6g
Cholesterol	0.0mg
Sodium	512.9mg
Carbohydrates	8.4g
Protein	6.7g

* Percent Daily Values are based on a 2,000 calorie diet.

FULL FALL POT ROAST

Ingredients

- 3 -4 lbs. pot roast, trimmed of fat
- flour
- 2 tbsp olive oil
- 2 C. sliced onions
- 1/4 C. water
- 1/4 C. ketchup
- 1/3 C. dry sherry
- 2 cloves garlic, minced
- 1/4 tsp dry mustard
- 1/4 tsp dried marjoram
- 1/4 tsp dried rosemary, crushed
- 1/4 tsp dried thyme
- 1 medium whole bay leaf
- 8 oz. mushrooms, whole
- 1/4 C. cold water
- 2 tbsp flour
- wide egg noodles, cooked and drained

Directions

- Season the roast with some salt and pepper. Dust it with flour.
- Place a large pot over medium heat. Heat in it 2 tbsp of olive oil.
- Cook in it the roast for 2 to 3 min on each side.
- Stir in the onion with 1/4 C. of water, 1/4 C. of ketchup, 1/3 C. dry sherry, 1 large clove garlic, minced, 1/4 tsp each of dry mustard, marjoram, crushed rosemary, thyme and 1 medium whole bay leaf.
- Bring them to a simmer. Lower the heat and put on the lid. Let them cook for 120 min over low heat.
- Drain the roast and place it aside. Discard the bay leaf.
- Get a small mixing bowl: Mix in it the cornstarch with 2 tbsp of flour.
- Stir the mushroom into the pot with the cornstarch mix. Let them cook until the sauce becomes thick.
- Adjust the seasoning of the sauce then spoon it over the roast. Serve it warm. Enjoy.

Servings per Recipe: 6

Timing Information:

Preparation	20 mins
Total Time	1 hr 35 mins

Nutritional Information:

Calories	128.1
Fat	5.4g
Cholesterol	0.0mg
Sodium	119.0mg
Carbohydrates	17.7g
Protein	3.0g

* Percent Daily Values are based on a 2,000 calorie diet.

SAUCY RED BUTTON SKILLET

Ingredients

- 1 tbsp oil
- 1 large onion, chopped
- 1 can button mushroom, rinsed
- 1 tbsp any soup mix
- 1 tsp paprika
- 1/2 tsp black pepper, grated
- water

Directions

- Place a skillet over medium heat. Heat in it the oil. Cook in it the onion for 5 min.
- Stir in the mushroom and let them cook for an extra 6 min.
- Stir in the soup mix with paprika, a pinch of salt and pepper. Cook them for 1 min.
- Stir a splash of water to make the sauce a bit thin. Let them cook until it becomes thick to your liking.
- Serve your cream mushroom warm with some rice, noodles or leftover meat.
- Enjoy.

Servings per Recipe: 6

Timing Information:

Preparation	5 mins
Total Time	25 mins

Nutritional Information:

Calories	32.0
Fat	2.3g
Cholesterol	0.0mg
Sodium	0.9mg
Carbohydrates	2.8g
Protein	0.3g

* Percent Daily Values are based on a 2,000 calorie diet.

Roasted Honey Mushroom Chicken

Ingredients

- 4 chicken breasts
- 1 medium red bell pepper, cored, seeded and strips
- 1 medium yellow bell pepper
- 1/2 lb. mushroom, cleaned and quartered
- 1 (14 oz.) cans diced tomatoes, drained
- 3 tbsp olive oil
- 2 tbsp balsamic vinegar
- 1 tbsp rosemary
- 1 tsp salt
- ground black pepper
- salt
- 1 1/2 tbsp honey

Directions

- Before you do anything, preheat the oven to 425 F.
- Get a baking dish. Combine in it the mushroom with tomato, bell peppers, olive oil, vinegar, rosemary, salt and pepper.
- Add the chicken breasts on top and press them into the mix. Sprinkle over them some salt and pepper followed by the honey.
- Place the dish in the oven and let it cook for 1 h.
- Serve your chicken and mushroom casserole warm with some rice.
- Enjoy.

Servings per Recipe: 4

Timing Information:

Preparation	10 mins
Total Time	1 hr 10 mins

Nutritional Information:

Calories	421.3
Fat	24.1g
Cholesterol	92.8mg
Sodium	685.0mg
Carbohydrates	18.0g
Protein	33.6g

* Percent Daily Values are based on a 2,000 calorie diet.

California Pizza Pan

Ingredients

- 1 1/2 tbsp olive oil
- 2 large onions, sliced
- 2 tsp honey
- 2 tsp balsamic vinegar
- 8 oz. fresh mushrooms, sliced
- 12 inches pizza crusts
- 8 oz. crumbled feta cheese
- 1 tsp dried thyme

Directions

- Before you do anything, preheat the oven to 450 F.
- Place a pan over medium heat. Heat in it the oil. Cook in it the onion for 11 min.
- Stir in the vinegar with honey. Cook them for 9 min. Stir in a pinch of salt and pepper to make the sauce.
- Lay the pizza crust on a baking sheet. Top it with mushroom, cheese, thyme, a pinch of salt and pepper.
- Place the pizza in the oven and let it cook for 16 min. Serve it warm.
- Enjoy.

Servings per Recipe: 4

Timing Information:

Preparation	10 mins
Total Time	45 mins

Nutritional Information:

Calories	260.7
Fat	18.1g
Cholesterol	53.5mg
Sodium	678.9mg
Carbohydrates	14.9g
Protein	11.3g

* Percent Daily Values are based on a 2,000 calorie diet.

GRATED SPUD AND MUSHROOM FRITTATA

Ingredients

- 2 large eggs
- 1 small potato, grated
- 1/4 C. cheddar cheese, grated
- 1 tsp dried chives
- 1 small tomatoes, diced
- 1 large mushroom, diced
- ground black pepper

Directions

- Before you do anything, preheat the oven to 350 F.
- Get a mixing bowl: Mix in it the eggs. Add the cheese with chives and potato. Combine them well.
- Place a pan over low medium heat. Coat it with oil and heat. Pour in it the eggs mixture.
- Lay over it the mushroom and tomato slices. Sprinkle over them some salt and pepper.
- Let it cook for 12 to 16 min. Serve it warm.
- Enjoy.

Servings per Recipe: 1

Timing Information:

Preparation	5 mins
Total Time	15 mins

Nutritional Information:

Calories	409.3
Fat	19.2g
Cholesterol	401.6mg
Sodium	333.3mg
Carbohydrates	35.1g
Protein	24.5g

* Percent Daily Values are based on a 2,000 calorie diet.

Thursday Morning Omelet

Ingredients

- 4 large eggs, beaten
- 1/4 C. cream
- 2 tbsp butter
- 1/4 lb. mushroom, sliced
- 1/2 garlic clove, crushed
- 1 pinch red pepper flakes
- 1/4 tsp thyme leave
- 1 tbsp sliced chives
- 1/3 C. Swiss cheese, shredded

Directions

- Get a mixing bowl: Whisk in it the eggs with cream.
- Place a pan over medium heat. Heat in it 1 tbsp of butter. Cook in it the mushroom with butter for 6 min.
- Stir in the thyme with pepper flakes and chives. Cook them for 30 sec. Pour in the egg mix.
- Stir them while cooking until they start to sit. Add the cheese and sit them until they are done.
- Serve your mushroom omelet warm.
- Enjoy.

Servings per Recipe: 2

Timing Information:

| Preparation | 10 mins |
| Total Time | 20 mins |

Nutritional Information:

Calories	415.2
Fat	35.5g
Cholesterol	452.2mg
Sodium	291.1mg
Carbohydrates	4.9g
Protein	20.0g

* Percent Daily Values are based on a 2,000 calorie diet.

TORTELLINI SOUP TOSCANO

Ingredients

- 2 tbsp butter
- 1/4 C. carrot, chopped
- 1 stalk celery, chopped
- 1 medium onion, chopped
- 1 tbsp garlic, minced
- 1/2 tsp thyme, minced
- 1 tsp Mrs. Dash seasoning mix
- 8 oz. sliced mushrooms
- 6 C. low sodium chicken broth
- 9 oz. 3 cheese tortellini
- 2 C. cooked chicken, chopped
- 2 C. baby spinach leaves, loosely packed
- parmesan cheese, grated

Directions

- Place a large pot over medium heat. Melt in it the butter.
- Cook in it the carrots, celery, onions, and garlic for 9 min.
- Stir in the mushrooms, fresh thyme, and Mrs. Dash. Cook them for 7 min.
- Stir in the broth and bring them to a boil. Stir in the tortellini with chicken.
- Let them cook for 8 to 10 min. Stir in the spinach and let them cook for an extra 6 min.
- Adjust the seasoning of your soup then serve it hot.
- Enjoy.

Servings per Recipe: 4

Timing Information:

Preparation	15 mins
Total Time	45 mins

Nutritional Information:

Calories	456.2
Fat	17.5g
Cholesterol	94.5mg
Sodium	633.8mg
Carbohydrates	41.0g
Protein	36.1g

* Percent Daily Values are based on a 2,000 calorie diet.

Herbed Mushroom Cakes

Ingredients

- 3 slightly beaten eggs
- 3 C. mushrooms, chopped
- 1/2 C. all-purpose flour
- 1/2 C. seasoned dry breadcrumb
- 1/3 C. onion, chopped
- 1 medium jalapeno pepper, chopped
- 1/4 C. parsley, chopped
- 1/4 tsp pepper
- 3 tbsp vegetable oil

Directions

- Before you do anything, preheat the oven to 350 F.
- Get a mixing bowl: Mix in the eggs, mushrooms, flour, bread crumbs, onion, jalapeño, parsley and pepper.
- Place a pan over medium heat. Heat in it the oil.
- Form 1/4 C. of the mushroom mixture into a cake and place it in the hot pan.
- Repeat the process with the remaining mixture. Cook them for 3 to 5 min on each side.
- Drain the mushroom cakes and repeat the process with the remaining mixture.
- Serve your mushroom cakes with your favorite toppings.
- Enjoy.

Servings per Recipe: 8

Timing Information:

Preparation	15 mins
Total Time	31 mins

Nutritional Information:

Calories	138.3
Fat	7.4g
Cholesterol	69.8mg
Sodium	161.3mg
Carbohydrates	12.8g
Protein	5.1g

* Percent Daily Values are based on a 2,000 calorie diet.

Steak and Potato Dump Dinner with Gravy

Ingredients

- 2 -2 1/2 lbs. boneless round steak, cut into 6 pieces
- 1 1/4 oz. dry onion soup mix
- 10 3/4 oz. condensed cream of mushroom soup, undiluted
- 1/2 C. beef broth
- 1 C. mushroom, sliced
- 1/2 C. onion, chopped
- mashed potatoes

Directions

- Stir all the ingredients in a slow cooker.
- Put on the lid and let them cook for 8 h on low.
- Once the time is up, serve your steak and mushroom gravy warm with some rice or noodles.
- Enjoy.

Servings per Recipe: 6

Timing Information:

Preparation	10 mins
Total Time	7 hrs. 10 mins

Nutritional Information:

Calories	69.7
Fat	3.1g
Cholesterol	0.0mg
Sodium	906.0mg
Carbohydrates	8.8g
Protein	1.9g

* Percent Daily Values are based on a 2,000 calorie diet.

Baja Mushroom Quesadillas

Ingredients

- 1/4-1/3 C. butter
- 2 -3 tsp chili powder
- 1 tbsp minced garlic
- 1 tsp dried oregano
- 10 oz. white button mushrooms, sliced
- 2 C. cooked chicken, chopped
- 1/2 C. onion, chopped
- 1/4 C. cilantro
- 3 C. cheddar cheese
- 16 corn tortillas
- olive oil
- salt and black pepper
- salsa

Directions

- Place a pan over medium heat. Heat in it the butter. Cook in it the chili powder, garlic and oregano for 40 sec.
- Stir in the mushroom. Cook them for 11 min. Stir in the chicken, onion and cilantro.
- Sprinkle over them some salt and pepper. Turn off the heat and let them sit for 22 min.
- Before you do anything, preheat the grill and grease it.
- Coat one side of 8 tortillas with oil. Lay them on a baking pan with the greased side facing down.
- Spoon into the mushroom and chicken mix. Cover them with the remaining 8 tortillas.
- Grease their top with oil and place them on the grill. Let them cook for 3 to 4 min on each side.
- Slice the tortillas into wedges then serve them hot with some sour cream.
- Enjoy.

Servings per Recipe: 1

Timing Information:

Preparation	25 mins
Total Time	31 mins

Nutritional Information:

Calories	378.6
Fat	23.4g
Cholesterol	86.0mg
Sodium	370.8mg
Carbohydrates	20.3g
Protein	22.9g

* Percent Daily Values are based on a 2,000 calorie diet.

CPSIA information can be obtained
at www.ICGtesting.com
Printed in the USA
LVHW101558130321
681463LV00003B/159